How To Not Be Toxic

The Ultimate Guide on How to Stop Being Toxic

Tom Pete

Table of Contents

Chapter 1

Understanding Toxicity

You've probably heard someone refer to another person's behavior as "toxic," or perhaps someone has accused you of being toxic on occasion. What are toxic personality traits?

Toxic traits are personality traits that are detrimental to other people, according to psychological experts. These are not infrequent actions. They are deeply embedded behavioral patterns that an individual exhibits time and time again. Chronic ways of feeling and thinking are also linked to toxic traits.

The thoughts, behaviors, and feelings that accompany toxic traits are harmful in the context of interpersonal relationships. Toxic characteristics can result in frequent conflict, bad relationships, wounded feelings, and even employment challenges.

While confronting other people's toxic traits can be challenging, the reality is that we also have to confront our toxic behavior. How can you tell if you have toxic traits? Think about whether there are patterns in your relationships. If several people have told you that your behavior is disturbing, it's probably time to explore whether there is any truth to what they are saying.

Think about recent conflicts you've had in important relationships. Have they all centered on the same issue? Perhaps several friends have accused you of being selfish, or maybe several relationships have ended because your ex-partner had problems with your negativity or judgmental behavior. Repeated problems in important relationships may be indicators of your toxic behavior.

Identifying Toxic Patterns in Yourself and Others

Part of understanding what toxic traits are is knowing the various traits that fall under the label of toxic personality traits. Below are several traits associated with toxic behavior:

Critical

People who tend to be critical tend to be overly critical of others. If another person makes a mistake, for example, they may pass harsh judgment and declare the person irresponsible, incompetent, or otherwise flawed, rather than giving him or her the benefit of the doubt.

Negativity

Negativity is often described as negative emotionality, and psychologists consider it a "dark personality trait." A person who displays negativity tends to experience a variety of negative emotions. Even when they are having a good time, they may appear melancholy, dissatisfied, or disappointed.

Lack of empathy

Empathy involves understanding another person's point of view and being able to identify with their emotional state. People who lack empathy seem unable to identify with the thoughts and feelings of others and may appear cold and selfish. Narcissism is frequently coupled with a lack of empathy.

Lack of responsibility

Lack of responsibility manifests itself when a person blames others for their problems and expects others to take care of major areas of their life. Someone who lacks accountability could neglect to pay their bills or complete their obligations and then blame you for forgetting to remind them of these things.

Greed

Those who are greedy are never happy with what they have. They constantly want to acquire more things, which may include designer clothes, expensive cars, or the nicest house in the neighborhood. People with this personality trait seem to be chronically dissatisfied and are more prone to aggression and negative emotions.

Gaslighting

Gaslighting is considered a form of emotional abuse because it involves one person trying to convince the other that he or she is crazy. He or she engages in manipulative behavior to try to make the other person feel crazy. For example, he or she denies having done or said things that he or she has done or said. Over time, this causes people to wonder if they are misinterpreting reality.

Dishonesty

Dishonesty is another dark personality trait. Dishonest people actively lie or hide the truth. When the truth is disclosed, this frequently leads to broken feelings.

Quick to anger

People who are quick to anger are often aggressive in nature. They are sensitive to imagined dangers and have a tendency to overreact when disrespected. Quick anger may manifest itself in the form of verbal attacks on others or physical aggression. They may also lack impulse control, causing them to respond swiftly and aggressively when threatened.

Selfishness

Selfish people do not care about the needs of others. In relationships, all decisions are centered on their preferences and desires. They are likely to disregard the opinions of others and do what is best for themselves, even if it harms others.

Cheating

People with the toxic trait of cheating believe they have the right to cheat in relationships. They convince themselves that if their partner is not perfect, they have the right to cheat to satisfy their needs. They might even cheat to punish their partner. For example, if their partner does not give them what they want or embarrasses them in some way, they may cheat in retaliation.

Jealousy

The jealous personality type is usually never happy because they constantly envy others. In relationships, jealous people find it difficult to be happy for their friends or important people because they are envious of their accomplishments. When you succeed or achieve something important, a jealous person will try to bring you down.

Stealthy

This personality trait is exhibited by people who conceal their genuine motives and conduct for their own gain. For example, they may badmouth a friend behind their back so that people will take their side and turn against their friend.

Impulsivity

Impulsivity is one of the toxic personality traits because people with a high level of impulsivity tend to be unreliable and have difficulty exercising self-control. A toxic friend may cancel plans at the last minute because something better has come up or may say offensive things in the heat of the moment because they have difficulty exercising self-control.

Laziness

People who have the toxic trait of laziness tend to be disorganized and don't do the things they say they are going to do. Research has shown that when people are lazy at home, they have less satisfaction in their relationship with their partner. A lazy person may not carry out household chores and is likely to expect others to take care of them.

Absolutism

Absolutists have extreme views and are intolerant of those whose views differ from their own. They find it difficult to compromise because they see the world in black and white. As absolutists believe that their way of thinking is the only acceptable way, it can be difficult to live with them.

The Impact Of Toxicity On Mental Health And Relationships

Relationships should lift our spirits, encourage us, and bring out the best in us, not the other way around. In a relationship, each partner complements the other. They stick together in good times and bad. They are there to help each other overcome their weaknesses and support their partner in achieving their dreams. But sometimes these relationships become the worst part of someone's life with their toxic imprints. Few people are aware that a toxic relationship can negatively affect their mental health and continue to suffer in silence.

Relationships that exhibit toxic dynamics are characterized by one partner consistently prioritizing their own needs and interests over those of the other. In a toxic relationship, each partner feels devalued and misunderstood. The partners often blame each other for the problems in the relationship, instead of recognizing themselves as the main source of conflict. They attack each other's character instead of addressing legitimate concerns or finding solutions.

The answer is nearly always yes if you ask yourself, "Can a bad relationship cause mental illness?"

Causes of toxic relationships

Toxic relationships are often the result of a combination of factors such as poor communication, unresolved personal issues, a lack of boundaries, and sometimes simply being with the wrong person. At this point, trust and emotional health are undermined as bad behavior patterns and treatment become the norm. These dynamics can develop slowly over time, so it's important to recognize the signs and take steps to resolve them to achieve a healthier and happier relationship.

The warning signs of a toxic relationship can include constant arguing, feelings of control, lack of trust, emotional or physical abuse, isolation from friends and family, and a general sense of unhappiness. This happens when the relationship constantly leaves the partner feeling exhausted, hurt, or trapped. Recognizing these signs of relationship toxicity is crucial to taking steps toward a healthier and more fulfilling relationship.

How toxicity affects relationship
There are those who are in relationships that function differently. They lose their identity. They feel dominated and the unsupportive partner puts unwanted pressure on them, which further leads to poor mental and physical health.

What most people don't know is how toxic relationships affect their mental health, and there is a deeper connection between unhealthy relationships and mental health.

When someone is in an unhealthy relationship, their partner traumatizes them to the point of bringing out the worst in them. Such a harsh relationship harms your physical and mental health and, over the years, it gets worse and worse.

Toxic relationships can have a significant impact on anyone's mental health in the following ways:

Anxiety
One of the most prevalent outcomes of toxic relationships in contemporary society is this. Relationships that are toxic frequently exhibit ongoing stress, uncertainty, and conflict phobia. Anxiety may rise as a result of this ongoing stress. People may have persistent anxiety, fretting about the upcoming fight or feeling uneasy about the status of their relationship.

Depression
Toxic relationships are emotionally draining and negativity can seep into your daily life. There can be feelings of sadness, hopelessness, and worthlessness. It can be emotionally draining to navigate a relationship full of conflict, manipulation, or abuse, which can contribute to depressive symptoms.

The results of this study's analysis also revealed that experiencing many forms of victimization in a relationship predicted an increase in PTSD and depression symptoms in individuals.

Low self-esteem

In a toxic relationship, individuals may be faced with continuous criticism, control, or emotional abuse. This may eventually undermine their sense of value and self-esteem. They may start to believe their partner's negative messages and question their self-worth, which can have a lasting impact on their self-image.

Stress

Constant stress in a toxic relationship can lead to chronic stress, which can manifest itself in physical symptoms such as headaches, muscle tension, or digestive problems. The stress hormones released in these situations can affect your physical and mental health, leading to exhaustion and burnout.

Isolation

Toxic partners can isolate them from their support system, including friends and family. Feelings of loneliness and a lack of emotional support may result from this isolation. Keeping up a strong social network is crucial since being alone can make a bad relationship worse.

Guilt and shame

Manipulative behavior in a toxic relationship can make people feel guilty and ashamed, even if they haven't done anything wrong. Manipulative partners often blame their partners, making them doubt their actions and intentions.

These feelings of guilt and shame can undermine their self-esteem and contribute to their emotional distress.

Physical health

The prolonged stress of a toxic relationship can affect your physical health. It can cause problems such as insomnia, high blood pressure, digestive problems, and even a weakened immune system. Our mental and physical health are closely linked, so pressure on our emotional well-being can manifest itself through physical illnesses.

Chapter 2

Self-Reflection

We all agree that removing toxic people from our lives is almost always a good idea. But what happens if you are that toxic person? We all have some sort of toxic habits. Some of us consciously feed them, but most of us feed them unconsciously. And, depending on how often we indulge in toxic patterns, these behaviors can become so ingrained that we are unable to see them. After all, once habits become secondary, they are difficult to unlearn.

Giving ourselves the time and space to reflect on what we show the world can change everything; that is, if we begin to do the work necessary to see ourselves clearly. Choosing awareness has the potential to transform dark habits into positive traits that can help us move up in life. But first, we have to turn the mirror around.

It's never easy or fun to do a serious self-assessment, but there's no other way to do it if you start to get the idea that the source of your problems may be you. When the same patterns began to follow me in my romantic and platonic relationships, I was forced to do some uncomfortable but very necessary work.

Along the way, I also realized that, as a society, we are very good at spotting the bad seeds and making the cuts we think are necessary. We often talk proudly about removing toxic people from our lives and encourage each other to do the same. But what happens when we dig deeper and realize that we are the biggest cause of our own unhappiness?

I know that while I was busy calling others toxic, I avoided facing my own demons. Blaming and finger-pointing was a seemingly safe way to distract me from what really needed to be looked at. This behavior was the result of a set of detrimental habits and patterns that I never felt "ready" to resolve. I had decided that this was who I was. It was my crutch for being a crappy person.

The simple fact that we are human means that, from time to time, we are going to struggle with negativity, either to give or to receive. The time when we need to start paying attention to this is when our negativity prevents us from improving our life situation. Identifying the signs is undoubtedly the hardest part. If you find it hard to take responsibility when something goes wrong, it's a sign.

Here's how to know if you need to analyze your own behavior and open yourself up to a detox:

You live for drama
It seems like you're always involved in some kind of drama. It haunts you wherever you go, but you don't know why you keep getting caught up in these situations.

While sometimes you can't help what's going on around you, it's completely different if you seem to be at your best when things go wrong. Drama is addictive. Reality television is a perfect example.

Getting excited about a dramatic existence will end up having consequences for you and those around you. Explore the reasons why this seems to be your favorite environment and take some time to identify the negative patterns that have become your norm. One possibility may be that you have always felt ignored and neglected, so creating chaos keeps you in the spotlight. Be willing to dig deep and root it out. Reach out to someone you trust or seek professional help and find productive solutions to get off this merry-go-round.

Your friends disappear
You may have noticed that people keep disappearing from your life without telling you why, stopping inviting you to things or making plans with you, screening your calls, or avoiding you. Be brutally honest with yourself about why your friends may be disappearing. Express your frustrations productively and set out with the intention of actually learning something about yourself, rather than setting yourself up for a fiery confrontation. If you're committed to taking back the relationship(s), start implementing real changes and breaking the cycles you've created.

You are a constant gossip
If you are constantly complaining about other people or criticizing the actions of others, you might want to take a look at your own actions. Human beings use gossip as a method of distraction from their own shortcomings and insecurities. We project onto others what we can't stand in ourselves.

If you have noticed that most of your conversations are filled with gossip and dissecting the lives of others, it is time for you to start working on it. Envy, jealousy, insecurities, and bitterness can easily turn into a destructive fireball, and gossip is just one of the many symptoms that this ball of doom spews forth.

Gossip is almost always negative, and these negative behaviors can be outrageously addictive. Have you ever noticed that sometimes it's much easier to point out something bad about someone than it is to bring their best traits to the table? That's how toxicity works, and it's present in all of us.

People often distance themselves from these types of individuals as a way to protect their privacy, their energy, and their space in general. It's very hard to trust someone who gossips constantly, because who's to say they won't talk about you the same way when they get the chance? Pay attention to the format of your conversations and how much of them revolve around talking about other people.

You are passive-aggressive
This is something I work on constantly. It's an easy way out when things aren't going so well: indirect hostility that manifests itself in the form of silent treatment, using stubbornness as punishment, blaming, avoiding, and withholding.

These tactics, among many others, form what we know as passive aggression. Tackling a problem as it is happening is something that many people shy away from. Those who have become accustomed to playing the role of "people pleaser" may even have an experience worthy of a resume in this area. Passive aggressiveness can quickly manifest itself in resentment and manipulation, and that's one place you don't want to go.

Talking can be difficult, it can even take some getting used to, but for any relationship to thrive, clear communication is imperative. Passive aggression can cause serious damage to a relationship if not dealt with properly, although some people see it as a defense mechanism to protect themselves and it can even originate in childhood. It's never too late to recognize it and do something about it.

If you're reading this and feeling a little triggered, maybe it's time to look in the mirror and start taking responsibility for your behavior. While the challenge may seem insurmountable, you'll soon discover that, ultimately, you're the one in control. And that's encouraging.

Understand The Roots Of Toxic Traits

Sometimes there doesn't seem to be any specific reason why a person acts this way; they just do. You may wonder why they are that way, so let's find out. Exploring the reason behind that behavior will allow us to build empathy through a better understanding of toxic people and perhaps can help us move forward and learn from toxic experiences. Here are some possible reasons why someone may have a toxic personality.

Before we go any further, let's remember that the goal of this book is not to attack anyone who exhibits the following signs, but to better understand them and draw attention to the reasons behind the behavior. If you identify with these signs, please do not take this commentary as an attack on your character. This book is intended simply as a self-improvement guide for those who feel stuck on this issue.

Insecurity and low self-esteem
Anger is often a response or expression of unpleasant emotions like rejection, grief, guilt, humiliation, or worry. When we feel insecure, belittled, or see ourselves in a negative light, we are more likely to project these negative emotions through toxic behaviors to regain control. Whether it's to promote our groups or ourselves, we tend to be more aggressive when our self-esteem is challenged and we don't feel particularly positive about ourselves. Essentially, we protect ourselves from becoming more vulnerable than we already feel by displaying unhealthy toxic traits.

Projection
People cope with negative views of themselves by perceiving that other people have particularly high levels of that same negative view. So basically, if you feel like you have a high level of anger, you are very likely to see that everyone around you does too, which makes you feel better about the issue you are having doubts about. Projection is the classic way someone can use this trait as a defense mechanism or distraction from the real concern at hand.

Feeling invalidated/unfairly treated
When you feel invalidated or suffer some kind of injustice, your anger is the emotion that speaks for itself. Your anger comes from a place of recognizing this injustice, which causes you to react to it. If you know someone in your life who shows signs of anger, which may include constant irritability, rage, stress, or frustration, this may be an indicator of how they feel about something. Perhaps they just want you to pay more attention to them because they feel lonely, or they

simply can't find a way to communicate their lack of satisfaction in an appropriate way.

Difficult childhood

Your childhood greatly influences who you are as a person. People who show signs of toxic behavior most likely had a difficult childhood, which may have included a difficult relationship with parents and siblings, as well as damaging characteristics of the environment in which they grew up. When you become an adult, you tend to carry with you the expectation of how you should cope with the negative feelings of your childhood. Some examples of how childhood negatively affects your behavior are having witnessed uncontrolled anger from your parents or other adults, or growing up thinking it was always right to act aggressively or violently. If you did not receive an adequate example of how to deal with anger or negative feelings in an emotionally mature way when you were younger, the struggle will weigh more heavily on you as you grow older.

Past experiences or trauma

Negative experiences from the past can have a great impact on our behavior, opinions, beliefs, and outlook on this world. A person who has suffered a significant amount of past trauma, abuse, bullying, or any other form of targeted behavior may have difficulty dealing with anger issues or toxic behaviors in the present, as they were not able to express themselves safely at the time. If you know someone who tends to struggle with these issues, it is likely that this behavior is a reflection of past struggles or challenges that have been behind them for years.

Current events that cause stress

Stressful circumstances in the present can be a major trigger for toxic behaviors. Perhaps you've been turned down for that new job, are experiencing financial difficulties, or have lost someone close to you. Situations that can increase stress levels can lead to anxiety, frustration, and feelings of being overwhelmed, which are more likely to be expressed through anger or toxic behavior. When someone is unable to figure out how to cope with stress, they may turn to toxic behaviors as a way to mask their internal concerns. When we are busy with too many stressful issues, our mind tries to filter them out, and the projection of that stress through toxicity kicks in as a coping mechanism.

Underlying mental health problems

Finally, if you or someone you know has been struggling with more severe or persistent signs of anger or toxic behavior in general, you should consider talking to a doctor or mental health professional, as the situation may have a deeper origin than you think. Persistent anger or frustration, along with unpredictable negative behavior, may be a sign of an underlying mental health problem or undiagnosed disorder. Be aware of the common signs of toxic behavior and, if you begin to recognize a pattern, it's best to seek help immediately.

Journaling and Introspection

One of the healthiest things you can do for yourself, especially during this turbulent period in your history, is to start journaling. This is not a "Dear Diary," but a deep look at yourself, what inspires you, what moves you, what scares you, how you can grow, and how to approach personal growth.

Journaling scripts can be very beneficial for those who are new to journal writing or don't know how to get started. They are also mindfulness exercises that can help you discover many things about yourself in ways you may never have considered, guiding you toward personal growth, self-reflection, and self-awareness.

Writing in a journal helps you get out of your logical mind and begin to explore your emotions, which are stored in another part of your brain. Writing by hand helps to activate the heart energy and your arms and hands are extensions of the heart energy. When you are grieving, journaling can reopen your heart and help you process your emotions so that you do not unconsciously externalize them to others in destructive ways. Journaling can also help you learn to set resolutions for the day.

Not everyone has time for this, and that's not a problem. A 2018 study found that even 15 minutes a day, three days a week of journaling can help with anxiety by giving your brain a healthy, positive boost, no matter what time of day you do it. Moreover, it might be a method to cultivate appreciation.

You don't need to sit down with a pen and paper - a journaling app works just as well - or write for hours or even every day to reap the benefits. For example, simply writing answers to questions about your relationship with alcohol can help you successfully get through a month without alcohol. Not writing in your journal for a few days may be honoring your intuition. You don't have to be hard on yourself if you don't keep a journal; self-compassion is important.

Speaking of intuition, you shouldn't feel limited to using only words. Putting down in writing everything you want, whether it's words, scribbles, or anything else, is cathartic. Writing in a journal is one of the ways children learn to understand their feelings and thoughts, and they are often encouraged to use words and pictures. In doing so, they can deconstruct what is going on inside them and get positive results.

Journaling Exercises for Self-Reflection and Self-Discovery

Here are some ideas for journaling to get you going:

- I'll break bad habits that don't help me.
-
- My presence on this planet is unique and significant because...
-
- When I'm feeling well, I encourage and motivate everyone around me by
-
- I've improved since yesterday since
-
- I ponder about it much too much.
-
- I'm proud of the way I carried myself when
-
- Because of this, I'm adding ______ to my bucket list.
-
- Love is best felt when...
-
- I feel most exposed when...
-
- Do I equate my value with significant achievements?
-
- I'm going to release what burdens me by...
-
- How can I continue to be open and attentive to the environment around me?
-
- What is my attitude about being a work in progress?
-
- I see remorse as looking like...
-
- I feel like ______ when I'm being who I am.
-
- My connection to honesty seems to be...

-

- I'm appreciative of the people I've met along the way because

-

- I get over my bad ideas regarding

-

- How does it feel to consider oneself to be a magnificent work that may never be finished—a magnum opus?

-

- Do I embrace change in my vision for the future, or do I run away from it?

-

- What was it that I was most struggling with last week? What advice would I give someone who was having the same issue as a mentor?

-

- What most satisfies me is...

-

- Do I think that other people inspire me just as much as I am inspired?

-

- Those who have most influenced my learning are...

-

- Do I feel sorry for those who have wronged me?

-

- To me, love seems to be...

-

- I live by the belief that every day has value and shouldn't be squandered. To that end, I...

-

- In ten words, I'm...

-

- In a nutshell, I'm not...

-

- I'll confront my anxieties bravely and with grace.

-

- I gave myself some alone time today by...

-

- Do I believe that life should be savored rather than hurried through?

-

- It overwhelms me when...

-

- I may set my limits first by...

-

- My favorite bodily part is...
-
- Do I have higher expectations for myself than I know I can sustainably give?
-
- Do I value the little things in life?
-
- I convey my self-love and self-worth by doing the following:
-
- My most recent dream that I can still recall was...
-
- They would think if my adolescent self met me today,
-
- I am aware of my advantages, which include
-
- I accept my shortcomings, which are
-
- Here's how my relationship with self-acceptance is going:
-
- I absolve myself of my...
-
- I pardon people for...
-
- I treat myself well when I
-
- Self-care feels and looks like this to me:
-
- I persevere because...
-
- I practiced awareness of myself and the people around me today by doing ______.
-
- Do I approach people and life in a varied manner?
-
- I discovered today that...
-
- I feel in control when...
-
- Am I afraid to ask for help?
-

- Do I feel I can be creative?

-

- Are there relationships in my life that do not satisfy me?

-

- Do I trust my intuition?

-

- I define emotional intelligence as...

-

- I welcome the future because...

-

- I am proud of...

-

- My relationship with trust is similar to...

-

- How do I feel about being empowered?

-

- I was more afraid when...

-

- Do I see challenges as enemies or as teachers?

-

- Do I feel that vulnerability is a weakness or a strength?

-

- My life took a significant shift when...

-

- I feel calm when...

-

- I feel happy when...

-

- What is the difference between listening and hearing?

-

- Do I permit myself to feel whatever I want to?

-

- Do I know my limits?

-

- What are the three things I appreciate most about myself and why?

-

- Do I feel I can take time for myself without feeling guilty?

-

- Have I been fully present today when?

-

- Do I feel that I am truly enough?
-
- How do I feel about the fact that I may be too much for some people?

Chapter 3

Cultivating Empathy

Empathy is the ability to see things from the perspective of others and feel their emotions. Putting yourself in another person's shoes can lead you to act with compassion and do what you can to improve your situation. In doing so, you can reduce the other person's distress and your own.

Imagine coming home to find that your spouse or partner is ill. Even if you were having a good day, you would suddenly feel their distress and attend to their needs. If a friend is angry at the way a boss has treated him or her, you are likely to share his or her sense of frustration. You may not be able to solve the problem, but you can understand that he needs to vent his emotions.

<u>Empathy is not limited to difficulties:</u> When your child is excited about something, you feel his joy. When your friend laughs at a joke, you feel his amusement. Empathy allows you to deepen your relationships, as you connect with the thoughts and feelings of your friends and loved ones, and they connect with yours.

<u>Empathy is not limited to those you know:</u> If you see someone sitting alone at a party, for example, you can empathize with their loneliness and talk to them. If you see images of others suffering on the other side of the world, you may be motivated to donate resources to help alleviate their suffering. On the other hand, when you see on television a crowd of people shouting for joy, you may feel your spirits lift. Their joy becomes your joy.

Here are way to cultivate it:

Practice listening
You can't put yourself in another person's shoes if you're not willing to listen to what they have to say. That's why the ability to listen is a vital part of developing empathy. You have to go beyond pretending to listen. The goal is to listen so carefully that you can understand the person's situation, points of view, and emotions.

<u>Identify and remove barriers to listening</u>: If you are stressed, you will find it more difficult to focus on the other person. Think about addressing the stressor-whether it's an impending deadline or a toothache before continuing the conversation. Multitasking is another common obstacle to active listening. Put away your cell phone and stop what you're doing so you can give your full attention to the other person. This is especially important in cases of disagreement or when dealing with sensitive or complex topics.

<u>Don't interrupt</u>: When you interrupt someone, you not only interrupt their train of thought, but you also run the risk of not understanding what they are trying to say. What's more, if you're formulating your next sentence while the other person is still talking, you're not listening at all.

<u>Don't judge</u>: If you know you disagree with someone, you may find yourself mentally disbelieving their words as they speak. It's advisable to listen with an open mind, however. Don't immediately criticize or blame the person as they speak, make an effort to comprehend their perspective.

<u>Let the other person know you are listening</u>: Nonverbal cues such as maintaining eye contact, and nodding your head, and verbal cues such as a quick "uh-huh" let the other person know that you have his or her attention. In essence, you are inviting him or her to continue. If you appear to be daydreaming or thinking about something else, the other person may interpret this as a sign that you don't care.

<u>Give your opinion</u>: If you think you didn't hear or understand something correctly, ask some follow-up questions. This way the person will be able to clarify his or her point of view, if necessary.

Read body language
Listening is not just about receiving verbal messages: people also convey information about their emotional state through nonverbal body signals. The ability to read body language is useful in all kinds of social situations.

Perhaps you have a friend who often says "I'm fine," but his or her grumpy expression tells you something is wrong. Or maybe you can gauge a date's interest in you based on the level of eye contact. ***People often convey messages through***:

<u>Facial expression</u>: Frowns, smiles, hesitant smiles and other facial expressions can convey a mood.

Eye contact: A person's eyes can be directed to whatever he or she is focusing on. Wide eyes can convey enthusiasm. Droopy eyelids may indicate that the person is tired or calm.

Voice: A person's tone of voice can indicate whether he or she is joking or serious. The speed at which he or she speaks can convey confidence or nervousness.

Posture: Stiff, tense shoulders can indicate apprehension. Relaxed shoulders and a hunched posture can indicate that the person is calm or bored.

Gestures: A lack of hand gestures may indicate shyness or awkwardness. A person who is relaxed and friendly may use his or her hands more. The speed and intensity of gestures can also convey aggression or excitement.

Not everyone uses the same nonverbal signals. And certain signals can mean several things. For example, is a person tapping their finger on the table because they're impatient or because they like the music playing in the background? Here's what to keep in mind when trying to understand someone's body language:

Look for consistency: Nonverbal clues need to correspond with spoken words. If your spouse says he or she is anxious, his or her fidgeting or frowning may reinforce this message. In situations where body language does not match what is being said, you may have to make a greater effort to understand what the other person is feeling.

Don't overemphasize individual signals: If you focus too much on a single signal, you are likely to misinterpret the other person. For example, someone looking away doesn't mean they are disinterested. They may simply be organizing their thoughts. When reading body language, look for multiple cues to gain a more complete understanding.

Remember that your nonverbal cues also convey messages to the people around you. If you are sitting with your arms crossed and looking away, the other person may interpret this as a signal that you don't want to talk.

If you want to encourage the person to talk to you, use positive signals, such as a friendly smile and relaxed eye contact, to project warmth. Learning to manage stress can help you avoid unconscious negative signals, such as frowning and maintaining a rigid posture.

Accept your vulnerability

Being empathetic requires you to show yourself vulnerable. When you hide behind an air of indifference, you make it difficult for others to trust or understand you. You also prevent yourself from feeling and understanding the full range of others' emotions. The following advice can help you open up:

Change the way you think about vulnerability: You may have been taught that it is a sign of weakness. Opening up to others, trusting that they will listen to you and accept your flaws, takes courage.

Speak up: Tell your loved ones how you feel. This requires reflecting on your emotional state and practicing openness with others. Be prepared to accept and communicate intense emotions, such as shame, jealousy, and hurt. The more you talk about your emotions, the more comfortable you will feel. You will also notice that others are more willing to open up to you.

Say what you need: Get in the habit of expressing your needs. Do you need someone to vent to? Or maybe you need assistance with something physically. It's better to discuss your needs with someone than to suffer in quiet. It not only simplifies your life but also gives your loved ones a sense of security and importance.

Take it easy: If you find it hard to talk about your emotions or express your needs, take it one step at a time. Maybe you could tell your friend about something that frustrated you about your day at work. You could also tell him or her about parts of your day that made you feel excited and happy. Or start by making a small request to your partner: "Can we take a walk together tonight? Walking helps me feel less stressed."

Don't focus too much on your reputation or your perfection: If you are too focused on how others see you, you may hesitate to be sincere. You may feel you need to create a facade to appear strong and carefree. Try to let go of this idea and start accepting your imperfections. Being honest will bring you closer to the people you care about.

Emotional Intelligence

Emotional intelligence, sometimes called emotional quotient or EQ, is your ability to identify emotions and use them to improve your life. For example, a person with a high EQ knows how to relieve stress and calm heated arguments. Emotional

Intelligence also enhances the ability to empathize with others, as it involves recognizing and understanding their emotions.

Self-management, self-awareness, social awareness, and relationship management are four characteristics of emotional intelligence. *Here are some tips for developing each of them:*

Improve your self-management skills by learning how to deal with stress: Stress can impair your ability to assess emotions and social situations, making it difficult to be present. Therefore, learning some stress-relieving strategies is an important step in improving your EQ. Practice relaxation techniques, such as deep breathing, which will help you stay calm in the moment. Other practices, such as physical exercise and meditation, are actions you can take daily to reduce your overall stress.

Increase self-awareness with mindfulness practices: Mindfulness involves focusing on the present moment but without judgment. You can use it to connect with and accept the emotions you are feeling at that moment. Are you bored? Are you anxious? Instead of labeling these emotions as "bad" or "negative," encourage curiosity about them. What triggers them? How do they make you feel physically? Do they affect your interactions with others? This practice can improve your ability to process emotions and increase your emotional well-being, in addition to increasing your self-awareness.

Increase social awareness by focusing on others: Mindfulness can also help you. Try to be present to the person you are interacting with. What is their body language like? Does a certain topic continually pop up? Relate this social awareness to your self-awareness. Is the person saying or doing something that stirs your emotions? Maybe their body language is soothing to you. Or maybe he or she is saying something that makes you anxious.

Use conflict resolution skills to manage your relationships: Even when you interact with your best friend or your closest family member, disagreements are likely to arise. You may have different opinions about politics. Or your plans for a vacation together may not coincide. Maybe one of you offends the other unintentionally. Knowing how to pick your battles, compromise, and forgive can help you overcome these inevitable conflicts.

New Perspectives
People are more likely to empathize with people who are similar to them. You may be more inclined to empathize with and assist someone who looks like you, acts like

you, shares your goals, or is experiencing similar difficulties. Unfortunately, this can lead to empathy bias when it comes to differences in factors such as race, religion, or culture. Here are a few strategies to combat it.

<u>Actively expose yourself to new perspectives</u>: If you're an atheist, attend a religious ceremony. Listen to podcasts that present a liberal viewpoint if you are politically conservative. If you're used to urban life, spend some time in rural communities. Look for common ground, but recognize the differences as well. You are not required to agree with every point of view. Spending time simply listening with an open mind, on the other hand, can help you see the humanity in people from different backgrounds or perspectives.

<u>Appreciate fiction</u>: Even knowing the perspectives of fictional characters can increase your empathy. When you read a novel, you try to understand a character's motives, goals, and emotional states. In other words, you exercise your capacity for empathy. The same is true when you watch a television show or movie with characters. Consider how you approach novels, films, and other works of art created by people from various cultural backgrounds.

<u>Be willing to challenge your assumptions</u>: As you interact with people from various backgrounds, you will likely discover that many of your assumptions about them were incorrect. It's fine to admit you were mistaken. Consider it a learning opportunity. You can also begin to challenge your assumptions in everyday situations. Perhaps your friend has a valid reason for being late. Perhaps the cab driver was rude because he was stressed. Think about "what ifs" to consider other viewpoints.

Empathy versus sympathy
Although the two words are often used synonymously, there is a difference between sympathy and empathy. Unlike empathy, sympathy does not involve sharing another person's feelings. When we sympathize, we care about the person's problem or misfortune and feel sorry for their suffering, but we do not fully feel their pain.

When a friend is grieving, for example, if we are sympathetic we understand why they are sad and grieving, and we feel their loss. However, if we are empathetic, we can also feel the pain they feel. Sympathy is more a feeling of pity for the person, while empathy is more a feeling of compassion for them.

The different components of empathy
Empathy often has at least two components, according to researchers:

<u>Affective Empathy</u>
The capacity to experience other people's emotions is known as Affective empathy. If your spouse is stressed and sad, you may mirror those emotions. If a friend is jovial and cheerful, you may smile because their happiness seems contagious. Jovial and cheerful, you may smile because their happiness seems contagious.

<u>Cognitive Empathy</u>
Cognitive empathy is the ability to recognize and understand another person's mood. It allows you to understand the other person's perspective and emotions. If you recognize that your partner is angry, you can predict that your joke is not going to go well. If you see that your friend is feeling helpless, you won't be surprised by his or her outburst.

These two components of empathy require different neural networks in the brain. Therefore, it is possible to have a lot of cognitive empathy but little emotional empathy, and vice versa.

Gender differences in empathy
Research shows that women are more likely to feel sad when they hear about the suffering of others. This is consistent with the results of a recent functional magnetic resonance imaging (fMRI) study, which showed that female brains appear to be more receptive to feeling the pain of others. However, the study revealed no sex differences in terms of cognitive empathy.

The Importance Of Empathy

Empathy plays an important role in life. First of all, it can bring you closer to the people you relate to. Trying to understand others, also makes them feel heard and understood. They are more likely to take the time to empathize with you as well. This deepens the relationship and fosters the sense of connection we all crave.

Studies show that having a strong social support network tends to increase people's happiness. Since empathy leads to better relationships, it can be a key component to building a more fulfilling life.

Motivating prosocial behavior: Empathy can motivate you to take actions that improve the lives of others. These actions can include anything from making a donation to a charity, encouraging a friend to seek help for alcohol abuse, or simply comforting someone with a hug.

Guiding decision-making: In social situations, empathy can help you decide what is the most sensible course of action. If your spouse seems stressed about work, you may deduce that it's not the best time to ask him or her to take on more responsibility.

Reduce burnout: The results of one study suggest that empathy can be helpful in reducing burnout. This is because empathy enables more effective communication and collaboration, even in difficult work environments.

Help alleviate conflict: If you have a bitter argument with a co-worker, for example, empathizing with him or her can prevent you from being overly critical or unnecessarily cruel. When you better understand the other person's point of view, it's easier to propose a compromise.

Creating empathy is certainly one way to expand your social circle and increase your happiness. But don't forget the benefits it also has for the people you meet. Empathy can have a cascading effect. By taking the time to listen to others, you're providing them with some level of emotional comfort. And you may be making it easier for them to trust, comfort, and empathize with even more people.

Chapter 4

Cultivating Positive Relationships

We all want to be happy, don't we? Happiness is a universal goal that motivates us to do many things. But what if I told you that cultivating positive relationships in your life could be the key to true happiness? Yes, you heard right. Creating and nurturing meaningful bonds with others can be a game changer when it comes to finding happiness and fulfillment. Let's explore how to discover the secret to happiness through the power of positive relationships.

The magic of relationships: Humans are social creatures, designed to thrive in communities and relationships. Whether with family, friends, partners, or even co-workers, the connections we make shape our experiences and our well-being. Bridging with others is like creating a support system that backs us up during difficult times and shares our moments of joy. So make it a priority to reach out to, engage with, and connect with people who bring you joy. Remember, happiness is contagious, and cultivating relationships is the key to spreading that joy.

Embrace genuine connections: In today's fast-paced world, it's easy to get caught up in the frenzy of amassing hundreds or thousands of online friends or followers. But it's not about numbers when it comes to relationships. The quality of those connections is what matters. Authenticity is the key ingredient in truly rewarding relationships. Invest your time and energy in developing genuine connections with people who value you for who you are. Look for people who inspire, support, and bring out the best in you. Remember that having a few close friends you truly appreciate is preferable to a large network of superficial acquaintances.

Surround yourself with good vibes: Have you noticed that surrounding yourself with negative people can drain your energy and lower your mood? Instead, spending time with positive, uplifting people can make you feel motivated, inspired, and happy. This is the power of positivity in relationships. Surround yourself with positive people who encourage and motivate you to reach for the stars. Avoid toxic relationships that depress you or drain your energy. Remember that your happiness is too valuable to be jeopardized by negativity.

<u>Give and receive:</u> One of the most lovely aspects of positive relationships is the opportunity to practice compassion. Compassion is the ability to understand and empathize with others, as well as to support and be kind to them. When we show compassion to others, we not only uplift them, but we also feel a deep sense of fulfillment in ourselves. So be there for your loved ones, lend a helping hand, and engage in active listening. Remember to allow yourself to be compassionate as well. When you need assistance, it is acceptable to rely on others. Sharing compassion in relationships creates a harmonious cycle of happiness.

<u>Keep memories</u>: Create meaningful experiences - Life is a collection of moments, and the memories we create with loved ones become treasures we keep forever. Make an effort to have meaningful interactions with the people who are important to you. Plan adventures, take up new hobbies together, or simply spend quality time enjoying each other's company. These shared experiences lay a solid foundation for lasting happiness and create bonds that stand the test of time.

The key to happiness lies in cultivating positive relationships in your life. Building bridges, embracing authenticity, surrounding yourself with positivity, cultivating compassion, and valuing meaningful experiences are the cornerstones of a fulfilling life. So invest in your relationships, spread love, and watch happiness find its way into your heart. Remember that the journey to happiness begins with the connections you make along the way.

Chapter 5

Practicing Gratitude

We are all capable of feeling gratitude, but sometimes we need a little reminder or coaxing to practice it. There are many reasons to practice gratitude, but only recently have we discovered one of the most important: its ability to change and strengthen the brain in extraordinarily positive ways.

Gratitude is powerful. It may not throw itself at our feet and demand our attention in a "why don't you notice me" kind of way, but it is powerful. Gratitude has been shown in studies to improve overall well-being, resilience, and social relationships, and reduce stress and depression. The more grateful people are, the happier they are and the more satisfied they are with life. They will also have a stronger immune system, lower blood pressure, sleep better (and wake up better). They will be more alert and more generous, compassionate, and happy. Grateful people are also more capable of feeling joy and positive emotions.

Gratitude involves noticing the goodness in the world, but it does not mean being blind to the difficult things or the turmoil that affects us all from time to time. Gratitude ensures that, in the midst of the things that bring us a good dose of negative feelings, we don't lose sight of the good. ***Here are some of the ways gratitude increases the volume of positive feelings:***

It strengthens our bonds with people
Gratitude is an acknowledgment that something important has been done for us. It is a deliberate and sincere acknowledgment of the generosity of the giver. Of course, we can also be grateful for broader things that have not necessarily been "given" to us by someone, such as our health, a safe place to sleep, or friendships. However, as with material things, showing gratitude for the less tangible things in our lives prevents us from being seen as "entitled" or as "parasites," which generally does not contribute to brilliant social relationships.

It lets people know that we are not the type to take things for granted.
There are two types of people. Those who wave to thank those who let them pass in traffic and those who do not. Each invites the world to give its own response.

Gratitude shows that it is good to relate to us and that we appreciate certain things without expecting them.

It reinforces generous behavior
Gratitude reinforces the generosity of both the giver and the receiver. When there is an open display of gratitude in our relationships, both people are more likely to repeat the act of giving and receiving. The effect of this attitude is not only person-to-person but can have repercussions in the world.

It increases feelings of security and connection
Gratitude helps us realize the good that comes from outside ourselves. We see the good in the world and in the people around us, which increases our feelings of safety and connection.

It sustains feelings of well-being for longer
Positive emotions tend to be like Teflon: they slip away from us too quickly. Gratitude allows us to hold on to the positive for longer and celebrate the good things in our lives that we would otherwise let slip away too quickly.

It eliminates negative feelings
It's hard to be appreciative and negative at the same time. The more space gratitude takes up, the more it will expand and give way to other positive emotions: connection, happiness, appreciation, and joy. More good feelings mean less room for toxic ones.

Helps fight depression
Research has found that gratitude can help fight depression and increase positive feelings.

Research has found that we tend to feel more grateful for experiences than for the things we have. There doesn't seem to be a clear reason for this, but one theory is that experiences are less likely to trigger social comparisons. While "things" may prompt us to compare what we have with what other people have, experiences are more likely to divert our attention to our personal circumstances and amplify feelings of appreciation, happiness, and satisfaction.

How Gratitude Changes The Brain

Parts of the brain that are activated when we feel grateful include the ventral and dorsal medial prefrontal cortex. These areas are involved in feelings of reward (the reward when stress is removed), morality, interpersonal bonds positive social interactions, and the ability to understand what other people think or feel.

Gratitude can also increase levels of important neurochemicals. When thinking changes from negative to positive, feel-good chemicals such as dopamine, serotonin, and oxytocin increase. All of these substances contribute to the feelings of closeness, connection, and happiness that come from gratitude.

Consistency

Gratitude builds itself. We know that the brain changes with experience, so the more gratitude is practiced, the more the brain learns to tune into the positive things in the world. This doesn't usually come naturally. Humans are prone to negativity, which means we are programmed to detect threats in the environment. This is good - it has kept us alive since the beginning of our existence - but in addition to being alive, we also want to be happy. When we focus too much on the negative, gratitude can be a way to nurture a more positive approach and teach the brain to spend more time feeling good and less time holding on to things that scratch us.

With the brain primed to fixate on the negative, we not only have to teach it to tune into the positive but also to hold on to those positives long enough for them to take effect. Our default position is to let the good things slip away quickly, so we have to be deliberate and hold on to them long enough to change the brain. Rick Hanson has done a lot of work in this field and has found that focusing on an experience for 20 seconds is enough time to create positive structural changes in the brain. Gratitude leaves room for the positive experience to expand, or for us to "re-experience" it, rather than forcing us to act quickly to overcome it.

Gratitude has the added power to initiate a social cycle that has the potential to expand the good for all involved. The more gratitude we feel, the more we will act prosocially toward others, which will foster their feelings of gratitude, which will make them more prosocial, and thus begin a beautiful cycle of gratitude.

How To Practice Gratitude

There are many ways to practice gratitude, but however you do it, it is important to do it with consistency and novelty. Our brains like novelty. In fact, they love it. They adapt quickly to anything that remains constant. That's why the joy we feel for things that initially drive us crazy quickly loses its luster. Our brains adapt, and when they do, they go in search of the next special thing. Gratitude can change this. With gratitude, we are constantly giving our brains something new and positive to focus on (as long as we practice gratitude for different things, not the same thing). Being grateful for the same things every day, even if they are important and worthy of enormous gratitude, will not have the same effect on the brain as finding something positive and new every time.

As for consistency, it seems easy enough to practice gratitude consistently, but if negative feelings tend to come up very quickly, it can be more difficult than expected. To avoid this, start with the little things. Things that require more effort will always seem farther away and more difficult. The harder they are, the less likely you are to accomplish them. Here are some other ways to practice.

3 things a day for 3 weeks

For three weeks, write down three things that happened in the last 24 hours that you are grateful for. These can be things in the world or things that have happened in your life, and they can be as big or small as you like - the breeze on your skin when you walk, the warm bed you sleep in, the coffee when you wake up. If you do this for 21 days, your brain will see the world differently. You will begin to examine the world and look for the positive aspects rather than the negative. It is important that the things you find in the world that you feel grateful for are new and concrete. Instead of "I am grateful for my friends" try "I am grateful for Max for making me laugh today."

Make the most of a positive experience

Whether it's a text message you received or a meeting with a person you like, find a positive experience and take two minutes to write down all the details. Write them down in a list and do this for three weeks. When you recall positive experiences, your brain marks them as important and the impression in your brain deepens. The brain does not distinguish between a real experience and a visualization, so remembering a positive experience after it has happened doubles the feeling of well-being in the brain. The idea is that after 21 days this becomes a habit and changes the way your brain sees and accepts the world.

Write letters

Spend a few minutes a week writing a letter to someone you are grateful to. It's entirely up to you whether or not to send it. The effect of this practice lasts for many months after the initial exercise. Researchers have described the changes in the brain as 'profound' and 'long-lasting'. One of the changes was a greater awareness of gratitude. This means that if we notice a good thing now, we are more likely to notice it later. This is how it works and practicing gratitude is a simple way to achieve this.

Gratitude rewires our brains to focus more on the positive aspects of the world than on our negative behavior. If we spend some time appreciating the positive, we will not become ignorant of the dangers, but we will become more open to what is good. Our brain will always look for things that keep us safe, but we also need things that feed our happiness and emotional well-being.

Conclusion

Finding fault with others or criticizing them is easy. But finding faults in ourselves is hard. It takes a lot of courage to admit that you are toxic. But when you accept it and are willing to work towards improvement, it becomes a truly commendable act.

A toxic person always causes harm to others. So now that you know you have some toxic behaviors, make sure you start taking serious action to stop being toxic. It is not easy to change yourself, but it is not that difficult either. I want you to know that by recognizing this point and getting to the end of this book, you have done something quite courageous. Not everyone can look at themselves and say, 'I need to change. I have to be better."

Self-realization is a lifelong journey. Hundreds of books and blogs have been written on the subject. Remember that you are not alone. By taking the necessary steps to become a better person, you are doing the work to improve your relationships too. This will be hard too, but by investing in yourself, you are also investing in these precious relationships.

www.ingramcontent.com/pod-product-compliance
Lightning Source LLC
Chambersburg PA
CBHW060904260726
48661CB00008B/3449